BLUE WINDOW 1911
MUSEUM OF MODERN ART, NEW YORK,
ABBY ALDRICH ROCKEFELLER FUND

COVER:

IN THE COVER PAINTING OF "BLUE WINDOW" HENRI MATISSE COMBINED A SERIES OF FORMS, CIRCLES AND TRIANGLES, WITH EXTREME CONTRASTING COLORS, BLUE AND GREEN, TO PRODUCE A SENSE OF UNITY AND WELL-BEING THAT CAN BE SEEN IN ALL OF HIS WORKS. MATISSE SAID, "WHEN I PUT COLORS TOGETHER, THEY HAVE TO JOIN IN A LIVING HARMONY, LIKE A MUSICAL CHORD. ALL MY EFFORTS GO INTO CREATING AN ART THAT CAN BE UNDERSTOOD BY EVERYONE."

BALLET DANCER AT THE MIRROR   1927
VICTORIA AND ALBERT MUSEUM, LONDON

BALLET DANCER REFLECTED IN MIRROR   1927
VICTORIA AND ALBERT MUSEUM, LONDON

LADY IN BLUE   1937   PHILADELPHIA MUSEUM OF ART: GIFT OF MRS. JOHN WINTERSTEEN

DEDICATED TO THE MEMORY OF ERNIE RABOFF AND TO FRED

NICHOLAS, PHIL LEVINE AND LUCKY ROBERTS WHO MADE

IT ALL HAPPEN..... AGAIN.

LIBRARY OF CONGRESS CATALOGING-IN-PUBLICATION DATA
RABOFF, ERNEST LLOYD.
    HENRI MATISSE.
    (ART FOR CHILDREN)
SUMMARY: A BRIEF BIOGRAPHY OF HENRI MATISSE ACCOMPANIES FIFTEEN COLOR REPRODUCTIONS AND CRITICAL INTERPRETATIONS OF HIS WORKS. 1. MATISSE, HENRI, 1869-1954 - JUVENILE LITERATURE. 2. PAINTERS-FRANCE-BIOGRAPHY-JUVENILE LITERATURE. 3. MATISSE, HENRI, 1869-1954 - CRITICISM AND INTERPRETATION-JUVENILE LITERATURE. 4. PAINTING, FRENCH-JUVENILE LITERATURE. 5. PAINTING, MODERN-20TH CENTURY-FRANCE-JUVENILE LITERATURE. [1. MATISSE, HENRI, 1869-1954. 2. ARTISTS. 3. PAINTING, FRENCH. 4. PAINTING, MODERN. 5. ART APPRECIATION] I. MATISSE, HENRI, 1869-1954. II. TITLE. III. SERIES: ART FOR CHILDREN.
ND553.M37R32   1988   759.4   [92]   87-16866   ISBN 0-397-32238-0
    "A HARPER TROPHY BOOK"   ISBN 0-06-446080-0 (PBK.)   87-17701

HENRI MATISSE

By Ernest Raboff

ART FOR CHILDREN

A HARPER TROPHY BOOK

HARPER & ROW, PUBLISHERS

HENRI MATISSE WAS BORN ON DECEMBER 31, 1869. HIS FATHER WAS A GRAIN MERCHANT IN LE CATEAU-CAMBRÉSIS, FRANCE, HENRI'S HOMETOWN. THE FUTURE PAINTER TURNED TO ART AS A PROFESSION AT 22 AFTER FIRST GETTING HIS DIPLOMA IN LAW IN PARIS. GUSTAVE MOREAU, A GREAT ARTIST-TEACHER TOOK THE 23-YEAR-OLD MATISSE AS A STUDENT IN 1892, WHEN HE GAVE UP HIS LEGAL WORK AND RETURNED TO PARIS. BY 1900, MATISSE WAS THE LEADER AND SPOKESMAN FOR A GROUP OF YOUNG POST-IMPRESSIONIST ARTISTS WHO STARTLED THE PARIS ART WORLD IN 1905 WITH AN EXHIBIT OF WORKS DEVELOPED FROM THE COLOR LESSONS OF IMPRESSIONISM, SIGNAC'S DOTTED POINTILLISM AND DIVISIONISM, VAN GOGH'S EXPRESSIONISM, WHICH A CRITIC CALLED THE PAINTINGS OF "WILD BEASTS" OR, IN FRENCH, "FAUVES." MATISSE WAS 50 YEARS OLD BEFORE SUCCESS ARRIVED. HIS WIFE, AMELIE PAYAYRE, AND HE HAD TWO BOYS AND A GIRL BY 1902. HIS WIFE MADE HATS, SHE AND THE CHILDREN WORKED AS HIS MODELS, SO HE COULD CONTINUE HIS CAREER. BY THE 1920s, MATISSE HAD INTERNATIONAL FAME AND IT CONTINUED TO GROW. HE DIED NOV. 3, 1954. HE REFINED THE JEWEL COLORS OF HIS TEACHER, MOREAU, AND THE "WILD BEASTS" INTO SIMPLE PAINTINGS OF GREAT PEACE AND BEAUTY.

MATISSE BY RABOFF

HENRI MATISSE SAID THAT IT WAS NOT THE FLOWER PAINTINGS AND LANDSCAPES HE LOVED TO DO BUT THE HUMAN FORM WHICH INTERESTED HIM MOST BECAUSE HE COULD USE IT BEST TO EXPRESS HIS RELIGIOUS FEELINGS ABOUT LIFE.

FOR HIM, AS MOST MEN, IT WAS THE FORM OF A WOMAN THAT HELD THE ANSWER TO THE MYSTERY OF LIFE.

WOMEN, ESPECIALLY HIS WIFE, AMELIE AND HIS DAUGHTER, MARGUERITE, WERE THE GOD-DESSES OF HIS FEELINGS OF LOVE. SO IT SHOULD BE FOR ALL MEN.

WOMEN WERE A BEAUTIFUL MYSTERY.

MY-STORY BY GOD!

HENRI MATISSE DEVOTED HIS LIFE AS AN ARTIST TO PAINTING THE LOVELY ASPECTS OF GOD'S STORY.

HE SAID, OFTEN, HE HAD A GREAT LOVE FOR PURE, SPARKLING COLOR, HE FELT HE HAD CONTRIB-UTED TO SOLVING PART OF LIFE'S MYSTERY WITH COLOR. HE CERTAINLY TAUGHT US ITS EMOTIONAL VALUE.

SELF PORTRAIT   1918   MUSÉE DU CATEAU

HENRI MATISSE SERVED HIS APPRENTICESHIP FOR 3 YEARS STUDYING IN THE STUDIO OF GUSTAVE MOREAU WITH FELLOW-STUDENTS, ALBERT MARQUET AND GEORGES ROUAULT. HE HAD A SOLID ACADEMIC TRAINING. HE LEARNED MUCH BY COPYING OVER 20 PAINTINGS (↑) BY OLD MASTERS SUCH AS RAPHAEL. HE LEARNED AND USED THE THEORIES AND TECHNIQUES OF THE IMPRESSIONISTS MONET, MANET, BONNARD AND VUILLARD. HE DISCOVERED JAPANESE PAINTING AND WOODBLOCKS. MATISSE WESTERNIZED ORIENTAL ART. HE EMPLOYED ALL AND EXTENDED THEM AS HE AND MARQUET BEGAN IN 1898 TO PAINT WITH BROAD STROKES OF PURE COLOR, EXHIBIT SUCH WORKS IN 1901, AND WITH OTHER FOLLOWERS, DERAIN, CAMOIN. VLAMINCK, MANGUIN, VALTAT, FRIESZ, PUY, AND ROUAULT, WHO HAD WORKED WITH THEM, THEY HELD A SHOW TOGETHER IN THE SALON D'AUTOMNE OF 1905 WHICH A CRITIC LABELED AS THE PAINTINGS OF WILD BEASTS (IN FRENCH, "FAUVES"). THE WORD HAS BEEN USED TO DESCRIBE THE MOVEMENT'S, OR SCHOOL'S, BRIEF HISTORY (1903-1907) EVER SINCE. MATISSE, ALONE, ITS FOUNDER AND MOST IMPORTANT MEMBER, DEVELOPED AND REFINED "FAUVISM" THE REST OF HIS LIFE.

WOMAN WITH THE HAT   1905   PRIVATE COLLECTION

THE SLAVE   1902-03
BALTIMORE MUSEUM OF ART

IN ADDITION TO HIS FORMAL ACA-DEMIC ART EDUCATION, HENRI MA-TISSE TURNED TO THE MASTERS OF HIS OWN TIMES TO IMPROVE HIS SKILLS. AUGUSTE RODIN WAS THE SCULPTOR WHOSE WORK INSPIRED HIS FIRST SCULPTURES LIKE "THE SLAVE." (←)

MATISSE'S SCULPTURE, HE SAID, HELPED HIM GIVE SOLIDITY TO THE HUMAN FIG-URES IN HIS PAINTINGS. HIS DRAWINGS ALWAYS CAME BEFORE BOTH. (→) THEY WERE THE SAME AS BLUE-PRINTS FOR THE ARCHI-TECT. FROM THEM, HE CRE-ATED SCULPTURES AND PAINTINGS TO LIVE FOR AGES. HE HAD STUDIED

TWO WOMEN IN STREET COSTUME
MUSEUM OF MODERN ART, NEW YORK

LAW. HE WAS A FINE MUSICIAN, A SKILLED VIOLINIST, A MASTER OF ALL THE TECHNIQUES OF THE ARTIST. LITHOGRAPHER, ETCHER, PAINTER, SCULPTOR.   MATISSE WAS CALLED "THE DOCTOR" BY HIS FRIENDS WHO ADMIRED HIS KNOWLEDGE, TALENTS, INTELLIGENCE, MORALITY, ETHICS, DIGNITY, AND ARTISTIC INTEGRITY.

JEANNETTE, I   1910-13
MUSEUM OF MODERN ART, NEW YORK
LILLE P. BLISS BEQUEST

EGYPTIAN CURTAIN   1948   PHILLIPS COLLECTION, WASHINGTON D.C.

THREE STUDIES OF ZORAH
ISABELLA STEWART GARDENER MUSEUM, BOSTON

CUBISM, CREATED BY PABLO PICASSO, ASSISTED BY GEORGE BRAQUE IN 1907, FRIENDS OF HENRI MATISSE, FATHER OF FAUVISM, BECAME A BRIEF, LOVELY, LEARNING PAUSE IN HIS CONTINUING EFFORTS TO EVOLVE FAUVISM FROM ITS EMOTIONAL YOUTH TO OBJECTIVE, MATURE AGE, ADULTHOOD. AFTER A TRIP TO MOSCOW IN 1911, AND JOURNEYS TO MOROCCO AND TANGIERS IN THE WINTERS OF 1911 AND 1912, HE, LIKE PAUL KLEE, AFTER A VISIT TO TANGIERS A FEW YEARS LATER, FELL IN LOVE WITH THE PURE COLORS OF ISLAMIC AND ORIENTAL ART. MATISSE USED THEM IN HIS OWN PERSONAL CONTRIBUTION TO CUBISM. HE TURNED PICASSO'S INVENTION, WITH ITS SOMBER GRAYS AND BROWNS, INTO COLORFUL, EYE-PLEASING ARCHITECTURAL CANVASES.

GOLDFISH   1915   MUSEUM OF MODERN ART, NEW YORK CITY,
GIFT OF FLORENE M. SCHOENBORN & SAMUEL A. MARX

PIANO LESSON   1916   MUSEUM OF MODERN ART, NEW YORK,   MRS. SIMON GUGGENHEIM FUND

PAINTING LESSON   1919   SCOTTISH NATIONAL GALLERY OF MODERN ART, EDINBURGH

"THE PAINTING LESSON" AND "INTERIOR WITH A VIOLIN" WERE WORKS EXHIBITING THE TWO SUBJECTS HENRI MATISSE LOVED THE MOST. WITH HIS VIOLIN, HE SOUGHT PURE, COLORFUL SOUNDS. WITH HIS PAINTINGS, HE TRIED TO CAPTURE AND HOLD A MUSICAL MOMENT OF BEAUTY IN TERMS OF LINES, FORMS, COLORS AND SPACE. (THE PAUSES BETWEEN OBJECTS AND THEIR COLORS, FORMS AND LINES.) IN 1920, HE DESIGNED A BALLET BY LEO-NIDE MASSINE, MUSIC BY IGOR STRAVINSKY FOR DIAGHILEVE'S RUSSIAN BALLET. YEARS LATER, IN 1938, HE AGAIN BROUGHT HIS LOVE OF MUSIC AND PAINTING TOGETHER IN HIS DESIGNS FOR THE SETS AND THE COSTUMES FOR MASSINE'S CHOREOGRAPHY, MUSIC BY SHOSTAKOVICH, FOR THE BALLET RUSSES DE MONTE CARLO.

INTERIOR WITH A VIOLIN   1917   STATENS MUSEUM FOR KUNST

WHITE PLUMES 1919 MUSEUM OF MODERN ART, NEW YORK

"WHITE PLUMES" DID NOT JUST HAPPEN. IT IS THE RESULT OF LONG, HARD STUDY AND WORK. MATISSE DID MANY PENCIL STUDIES FOR HIS PAINTINGS SO THAT THEY WOULD BE LIKE MUSIC TO THE EYES. THE **COLOR** OF DRESS FILLS THE CANVAS WITH LIGHT. THE MODEL'S CONCENTRATION ON HER JOB IS READ ON THE EXPRESSION OF HER FACE. THE WHITE PLUMES, THE FEATHERS THAT BRIM HER HAT REPEAT THE FULL CURVES OF HER HAIR. THE V OF HER

WHITE PLUMES 1919 BALTIMORE MUSEUM OF ART

DRESS POINTS TO THE BLACK BELT, ALMOST CONCEALED IN ITS FOLDS, LEADING ONE'S GAZE BACK TO THE HEAD. THE RICH, VELVETY RED BACKGROUND IS A BRILLIANT SETTING FOR THE OTHER JEWEL-LIKE COLORS WITH HER LIPS RETURNING OUR ATTENTION TO HER INTEREST-ING EXPRESSION. MATISSE IS A MASTER COMPOSER WITH PAINT.

PLUMED HAT 1919 DETROIT INSTITUTE OF ARTS

WHITE PLUMES   1919   MINNEAPOLIS INSTITUTE OF ARTS, WILLIAM HOOD DUNWOODY FUND

MUSIC LESSON 1917 BARNES COLLECTION

HENRI MATISSE'S LIFE WAS CENTERED AROUND HIS FAMILY. LIKE CRAFTSMEN AND ARTISTS OF OLD, HE SHARED MOST OF HIS TIME AND TALENT WITH THEM. HE PAINTED THEM FREQUENTLY, AS IN THIS DETAIL (←) FROM THE MUSIC LESSON.
MOST FAMILIES BEFORE THE INDUSTRIAL-TECHNOLOGICAL AGE LIVED AND WORKED TOGETHER, MATISSE UNDERSTOOD THE IMPORTANCE OF THAT TRUTH.
IN HIS ORDERING OF VALUES AND PRIORITIES, HE WAS A HUSBAND, FATHER, BREADWINNER IN THAT ORDER. SUCH ARE THE DECISIONS A THOUGHTFUL INTELLIGENT MAN CAN MAKE, AS MATISSE PROVED, EVEN LATE IN THE 20th CENTURY. MEDITATION (→) SHOWS AMELIE MATISSE, WIFE, MOTHER AND MODEL FOR HER HUSBAND, POSING IN HER ROBE, FRESHLY-WASHED HAIR WRAPPED IN A TOWEL, DEEPLY CONCENTRATING ON HER OWN THOUGHTS. THE PORCELAIN

PIANO LESSON 1923 SCOTTISH NATIONAL MUSEUM

VASE AND FLOWERS ON THE CANDY-STRIPED TABLE-CLOTH LOOK LIKE A PRESENT, A SYMBOL OF NATURAL BEAUTY TO THE WIFE HE RESPECTED AND ADMIRED, THE TWO SIDES OF THE COIN OF LOVE.

MEDITATION   1920   PRIVATE COLLECTION

MADAME MATISSE 1903
STATENS MUSEUM FOR KUNST

MARGUERITE 1906 PEN AND INK

(←)MADAME MATISSE AND HER DAUGHTER(↑) AND TWO SONS OFTEN WERE PATIENT MODELS FOR HUSBAND AND FATHER, HENRI MATISSE. HIS WIFE'S PORTRAIT, AND THE PAINTING BELOW, SHOW VINCENT VAN GOGH'S INFLUENCE IN THE USE OF RAW PURE COLOR TO CREATE EMOTIONAL REACTIONS.

STILL-LIFE WITH RED CARPET 1906 MUSÉE DES BEAUX-ARTS, GRENOBLE

SEATED ODALISQUE   1928   BALTIMORE MUSEUM OF ART

WOMAN 1910 PEN AND INK

HENRI MATISSE HAD THE GOOD FORTUNE OF HAVING PUBLISHERS OF HIS BOOK ILLUSTRATIONS WHO UNDERSTOOD THAT A BOOK MUST BE DESIGNED AS CAREFULLY AND CREATIVELY AS A PAINTING. "I DO NOT DIFFERENTIATE BETWEEN THE CONSTRUCTION OF A BOOK AND THAT OF A PICTURE, AND I PROCEED ALWAYS FROM THE SIMPLE TO THE COMPOSITE... THE PROBLEM OF BALANCING THE TWO PAGES(↓)." THE PAGES OF THIS BOOK ILLUSTRATE THIS PROBLEM AND THE SOLUTION TO GIVE BALANCE, PURPOSE AND MEANING (LIFE) TO THE TEXT FACING MATISSE'S MAGNIFICENT, BEAUTIFUL, AND SIMPLE, EASILY UNDERSTOOD FORMS AND PURE COLORS. FLOWERS AND LEAVES, LIKE A WOMAN IN A LOVELY DRESS APPEAR MORE AND MORE FREQUENTLY FROM THE 1930's TO THE END OF MATISSE'S LIFE. HE SOUGHT "MUSICAL-HARMONY" IN THEIR LINES, FORMS, AND COLORS, GIVING LIVING, BREATHING-ROOM TO ALL THINGS IN NATURE'S SPACE.

POÉSIES BY MALLARMÉ 1932

MUSIC   1939   ALBRIGHT-KNOX ART GALLERY, BUFFALO

THERE IS A SAYING "GENIUS IS 99% HARD WORK, 1% INSPIRATION." HENRI MATISSE KNEW THAT THE "INSPIRATION" WAS ANOTHER WAY OF SAYING "SEE WHAT HAS TO BE DONE BY STUDYING THE PROBLEM, OBJECTIVE OBSERVATION, UNTIL ONE ACHIEVES AN EASY, DIRECT, WORKABLE SOLUTION." HE PAINT-ED WITH THE CLINICAL ATTITUDE

SELF PORTRAIT   1900   BRUSH AND INK

OF A SURGEON, THE CONCENTRATION OF A PILOT LANDING A JET AIRLINER, THE LOVE OF A FATHER TEACHING HIS CHILD HOW TO WALK, OR A MOTHER CHANGING HER BABY'S DIAPERS. GENIUS IS THE ABILITY TO WORK OBJECTIVELY WITH LOVE FOR SOLVING DIFFICULT PROBLEMS AND CHORES, MENIAL OR MENTAL, BY THE MOST EFFICIENT, ECONOMIC, AND PRO-DUCTIVE LABOR. MATISSE DID STUDY AFTER STUDY TO ELIMINATE WHAT WAS UNESSENTIAL IN HIS SEARCH FOR TRUTH AND BEAUTY. BELOW ARE JUST A FEW THAT LED TO HIS FINAL VERSION OF THE PAINT-ING OF ROUMANIAN BLOUSE.

STUDIES OF ROUMANIAN BLOUSE   1939-40

ROUMANIAN BLOUSE   1940   MUSÉE NATIONAL D'ART MODERNE

HENRI MATISSE SOUGHT WOMEN, THEIR MYSTERY, THEIR MAGIC, *THEIR* BEAUTY, AND, ABOVE ALL ELSE, HIS RELIGIOUS ATTITUDE TOWARDS THEM IN THE HUNDREDS OF DRAWINGS, ETCHINGS, LITHOGRAPHS, LINOLEUM CUTS, COLLAGES, SCULPTURES AND PAINTINGS MADE THEM RESEMBLE GODDESSES. HE WAS ORIENTAL IN HIS REGARD FOR THEM.

WHITE FRILLS   1936
BALTIMORE MUSEUM OF ART

MATISSE LOVED THEIR PASSIVITY, DAY-DREAMING, THEIR COMPLETION, FULFILLMENT OF A MAN WHO ACCEPTED THEM AS THEY WERE, AS WOMEN. ALL WOMEN WERE POTENTIALLY MADONNAS. IT IS A MAN'S INTELLIGENCE, FEELINGS, ACTIONS, BEHAVIOR TOWARDS THEM WHICH HELPS THEM TO REALIZE THOSE POSSIBILITIES. A MAN MUST BE, AT ONE AND THE SAME TIME, HUSBAND, LOVER, FATHER, BROTHER, FRIEND, DOCTOR, AND, ESPECIALLY, TEACHER FOR HIS WIFE. SHE MUST FILL FOR HIM EQUAL ROLES AS A WOMAN. MATISSE'S UNDERSTANDING OF THOSE TRUTHS IS IN HIS WORK. HE USED LINE, FORM, COLOR, SPACE AS WORDS, SENTENCES, PARAGRAPHS, CHAPTERS, TO "WRITE" HIS PHILOSOPHY ABOUT THEM IN HIS PAINTINGS.

THREE SISTERS   1916   MUSÉE DE L'ORANGERIE

JOAQUINA   1911   PRAGUE, NARODNI GALERIE

HENRI MATISSE REMAINED A FAUVE ALL OF HIS LIFE. HE BECAME A SCIENTIST OF PURE COLORS. HE USED THEIR STORY-TELLING STRENGTH LIKE THE JAPANESE WOODBLOCK ARTISTS HE LOVED AND WHOSE WORK HE COLLECTED.

THE FAIR TAHITIAN WOMAN 1938 LINOLEUM CUT

LIKE MANY PAINTERS OF THE 20th CENTURY, HE RECOGNIZED, FROM THE PAINTINGS OF HIS OWN CHILDREN, THIS ORIENTAL USE OF PURE RED TO SHOW HEAT, ACTION, EXCITEMENT, FIRE OR SUNLIGHT; ORANGE TO BRING THE EMOTIONS OF LOVE, TENDERNESS, THE FEMALE, FELINE QUALITIES INTO THINGS LIKE THE SHAPE OF A VASE, A CAT, A WOMAN OR A MAN. HE UNDERSTOOD BLUE WAS THE COLOR OF THINGS WHICH ARE ABOVE. THE RED EARTH, ABOVE FEELINGS. IT WAS THE COLOR SHOWING THOUGHT, PROPER BEHAVIOR, THE MIND, SKIES OR HEAVEN. THE COLORS GIVE MEANING TO THE LINES. THE LINES REVEAL THE PURPOSE, THE USE OF THE FORM. EVERY THING, EVERY-BODY (FORM), NEEDS ITS, HERS OR HIS OWN SPACE IN WHICH TO LIVE · BE · BREATHE (ACT · FEEL · THINK). HENRI MATISSE, A PHILOSOPHER OF COLOR, CHOSE THE SIMPLE LINES OF A CHILD TO HELP US "READ" WHAT HE THOUGHT.

LARGE RED INTERIOR   1948   MUSÉE NATIONAL D'ART MODERNE

CHAPEL OF THE ROSARY   1950   VENCE

FROM 1947 TO 1951, MATISSE CREATED THE ONLY RELIGIOUS COMMISSION OF HIS LIFE FOR A DOMINICAN ORDER IN VENCE, FRANCE. IN A MESSAGE HE SENT AT ITS DEDICATION, HE WROTE "......I CONSIDER IT MY BEST PIECE OF WORK. I HOPE THAT THE FUTURE WILL JUSTIFY THIS OPINION BY A GROWING INTEREST." HE WANTED IT JUDGED AS "THE RESULT OF A LIFETIME DEVOTED TO THE SEARCH FOR TRUTH." THE WHITE-WALL-MURALS ARE DRAWN WITH BLACK PAINT LIKE PRE-HISTORIC ROCK AND CAVE PICTOGRAPHS. THEY ARE SIMPLE AS A CHILD'S AND EASILY UNDERSTOOD BY VISITORS FROM AROUND THE WORLD. THE CHAPEL BRINGS PEACE, SERENITY AND QUIET BEAUTY TO ITS BEHOLDERS.

STATIONS OF THE CROSS   1949-50   VENCE

INTERIOR OF CHAPEL OF THE ROSARY   1950   VENCE

RECLINING NUDE III   1929   BALTIMORE MUSEUM OF ART